The
ART
of
BEING
a
HEALING
PRESENCE

BOOKS BY JAMES E. MILLER

Change & Possibility
Autumn Wisdom
The Caregiver's Book
When You Know You're Dying
One You Love Is Dying
When You're Ill or Incapacitated/When You're the Caregiver
What Will Help Me?/How Can I Help?
How Will I Get Through the Holidays?
Winter Grief, Summer Grace
A Pilgrimage Through Grief
Helping the Bereaved Celebrate the Holidays
Effective Support Groups
The Rewarding Practice of Journal Writing
One You Love Has Died
When Mourning Dawns
Finding Hope (with Ronna Jevne)
The Gift of Healing Presence
This Time of Caregiving
The Art of Listening in a Healing Way

The ART of BEING a HEALING PRESENCE

A Guide for Those in Caring Relationships

James E. Miller

with

Susan C. Cutshall

WILLOWGREEN® PUBLISHING

To the founders and staff
of GilChrist Contemplative Retreat Center,
Three Rivers, Michigan for their quiet, loving hospitality,
allowing others to sink more deeply into the mystery of life,

and

To the patients, families and staff of Franciscan Hospice Service,
Tacoma, Washington for their teachings about courage, dignity
and love in the face of the mystery of death.

Copyright 2001, 2012
by James E. Miller

Willowgreen Publishing
10351 Dawson's Creek Boulevard, Suite B
Fort Wayne, Indiana 46825
260/490-2222

Library of Congress Control Number: 2001093357

ISBN 978-1-885933-32-4

The scholar seeks,
the artist finds.

ANDRÉ GIDE

TABLE OF CONTENTS

FOREWORD

When I think about healing presence, I remember Tom. Tom and I were in graduate school together. He was married, and I was engaged to be married very soon. At dinner in a restaurant one Friday evening, my fiancée announced that she wasn't sure she wanted to marry me. I was stunned. A few hours later, leaving behind a short note and her engagement ring, she left. For several days, no one knew where she was.

I was devastated. I was scared for her; I was miserable and grieving myself, barely managing to get through each day. During that period I occasionally asked Tom if I could talk with him. He would invite me over to his small apartment, shooing his family away so we could have privacy, and then he'd sit and listen.

Thinking back about those talks, I realize that Tom said very little. He did very little. And yet what a difference he made for me. I also now realize how difficult those talks must have been for Tom. As a Marine sergeant in Viet Nam, he was an action-oriented fellow who wanted and expected results. But in this case he couldn't produce results. He couldn't bring my fiancée back; he couldn't take away my pain; he couldn't explain to me why she had done this.

Yet more than anyone else at that critical time in my life, Tom was a healing presence. Because he listened to my repetitive talking with such patience, I was able to say what I needed to say. Because he accepted me in my brokenness with such compassion, I was better able to accept and work through my brokenness myself. Because he believed in me, because he believed the universe was ultimately trustworthy, then little by little I could believe it, too. Tom, more than anyone, helped me begin to heal.

Perhaps you have known someone like Tom in your life. Perhaps you've had a similar experience of healing and growth. That's what this book is about—how we can be present to one another so that these kinds of experiences can be encouraged and nurtured. Whether or not you have *known* someone like Tom, there is always an invitation to *be* someone like him.

If you stop to be kind,
you must swerve often from your path.

MARY WEBB

3

Let your love be like misty rain:
gentle in coming but flooding the river.

AFRICAN PROVERB

3

To yield is to be preserved whole.
To be bent is to become straight.
To be empty is to be full.
To be worn out is to be renewed.

LAO TSU

1

When you're a healing presence, you're an artist.

A nurse washes the body of a stillborn child, then wraps and brings the baby to the mother and father. She models for them the naturalness of holding their child as they say their goodbyes. She stays close for awhile, then she recedes, allowing their privacy. Later, she is quietly available as the parents make plans for what they will do next. That is healing presence.

A volunteer for his congregation visits a man whose wife has Alzheimer's Disease. The husband talks about the stress of his full-time caregiving responsibilities. He voices his sadness, anger and loneliness, as well as his guilt for having some of these feelings. The volunteer listens thoughtfully, nodding from time to time. When he finally speaks, he acknowledges the husband's feelings, then reports what he is witnessing: a loving husband who provides excellent care in very trying circumstances. Tears of relief and appreciation form in the husband's eyes as the two sit quietly. That is healing presence.

An aide bathes an elderly woman who lies in a nursing home bed. The woman seems alert but cannot speak. With great care the aide gives the woman a bath and shampoos her hair, talking softly, moving gently. Tasks complete, the aide sits for a few moments beside the woman's bed, holding and stroking her hand. That is healing presence.

A hospice social worker enters the bedroom of a man who lies dying, surrounded by anxious family members. She kneels beside his bed, takes his hand and asks, "Would you like me to tell you what I see?" With his consent, she tells him she senses his struggle. She sees also that his disease is becoming larger than his ability to fight it. With direct and tender words, she speaks the truth of his approaching death. Her quiet honesty disarms all defenses, enabling the man and his family to take a step beyond their fear and begin facing the pain of their approaching losses. She continues to kneel there as emotion fills the room. That is healing presence.

The members of a support group listen in respectful silence as a man stammers out the story of his abuse as a child. In another group, members hold their breath as a fellow breast cancer survivor reports on an appointment with her oncologist, then they celebrate together upon hearing good news. Sitting in their living room, a man shares a cup of coffee with his wife at the end of their workday, listening carefully as she tells the involved story of a painful encounter with a co-worker. These, too, are examples of healing presence.

What healing presence is.

Healing presence is the condition of being consciously and compassionately in the present moment with another or with others, believing in and affirming their potential for wholeness, wherever they are in life.

As this definition implies, healing presence doesn't entail much activity. While it can make a major difference in people's lives, as it's taking place, it may appear that very little is happening. While healing presence is a powerful gift, you don't have to be expertly trained or well educated to companion another in this way. In fact, training and education may sometimes get in the way.

Healing presence requires a certain amount of time, yet its effects may be evident very rapidly, perhaps immediately. It can take place while other things are going on. You can be a healing presence, for example, while performing a medical procedure, as you're caring for others' physical, emotional, or spiritual needs, while you're working beside them, or as you're just enjoying another's company. You can certainly be a healing presence with someone you know well, and you can be equally effective with someone you've never met before, or someone you'll know only briefly. The possibilities are limitless.

What this book will offer.

In the pages that follow, we will explore this art of being a healing presence. The information will be placed in a form general enough to apply to many different personal situations and work environments. At the same time, it will be specific enough that you will be able to use these ideas however you live and wherever you work.

As the title of this book implies, healing presence is an art, not a science. In any artistic field, there are universal principles that hold. Yet all artists apply these principles in their own way, making their work personal and distinctive, combining their intuition and vision with their gifts and skills to create something uniquely theirs.

This is how it is with healing presence. We are all invited to bring our uniqueness, our depth, and our fullness to this creative undertaking—to put our own signature on being a healing presence.

The most beautiful music of all
is the music of what happens.

IRISH PROVERB

To live is so startling
it leaves little time for anything else.

EMILY DICKINSON

To wonder is here, not there.
Now, not to be.
Now always.

RICHARD JEFFRIES

2

Being present is simple, but that doesn't mean it's easy.

Being present is not a complicated matter—all you do is wake up.
You open your eyes, look around, and come to your ordinary senses.
Once you are awake, you stay that way as long as you can.

You wake up to where you are, taking in all that is around you.
Sometimes you survey the entire panorama. Other times you focus
on the details, paying attention to lines, shapes, colors, textures.
Following your natural curiosity, you open to as much as possible.

You wake up not just to your surroundings but to what is going
on in those surroundings. Is there movement? Where? What sort?
Is there stillness? What is its quality? Are there sounds? How many?
What kind? What do your senses gather and convey?

Being really present includes being awake to yourself. What is
happening within you while other things are happening around you?
What is your body telling you? What are you feeling? What are you
thinking? Another person or other people may be present, so you
awaken to them, too. Who are they? What are they like? What are
they doing? What is occurring between you?

When you are completely present, you stay awake to each unfolding
moment. You give yourself fully to the present instant, letting go of
what was, and choosing not to anticipate what will be.

You don't *do* presence—you *are* presence. It's as simple as that. Nevertheless, it is not necessarily easy, for in today's world, most of us are busy—too busy. We jump from one thing to another, often without pausing. We do two things at once, if not three or four. Many of us are constantly balancing demands at work with responsibilities at home, what we *have* to do with what we *want* to do. We overfill our days with activities until these activities overfill us.

Is it any wonder that our minds become so scattered? Without intending to and often without being conscious of doing so, we are engaged in a non-stop chatter that circles inside our heads. We make judgments, stage arguments, create rationalizations and rehearse conversations in our minds hour after hour. When so much is going on within us, we are distracted from what's going on around us, and consequently we are in danger of being more absent than present.

This "multi-tasking" attitude that we fall into in everyday moments and workaday situations can interfere with our simple presence. We unthinkingly assume these moments are so ordinary that we take them for granted. We see a tree or the sky or a particular person so many times, day after day, that we forget. We forget how amazing a tree really is, how truly spectacular the sky can be, and the unique miracle of this other being. We lose sight of the extraordinary as it lies hidden in what we call the ordinary. Once we allow that to happen, it is difficult to reawaken, to consciously rediscover the wonderment and the vitality around us.

A strong desire to act, to be effective, can also hinder being present. We want to exert our influence upon the world, and so rather than allowing ourselves to stay with the moment, we swing into action. We hurry to *do* something with that moment. Applying skills we've developed, we make something happen. Wanting *our* expectations to be fulfilled, we do what we can to influence the outcome.

When we become locked into living our days in this way, it's difficult to stop. Our culture rewards our being effective more than it does our being mindful, our being assertive over our being awake. Yet if we're going to be fully present, this is our invitation—we're asked to awaken and to stay awake. This is not a once-and-for-all experience. We shall awaken many times and we shall call ourselves back to wakefulness many more.

Sometimes it will feel natural to stay present in this way, although it may still not be easy. We will have to persist in quieting our mind's chatter if we want to really hear what another person has to say. This takes discipline and effort. We will be called upon to use our senses, our intuition, and our whole body in ways that perhaps are not yet fully developed. Yet the more we practice being completely present, the more natural it becomes. The more we wake up to what is around us and within us, the more we are inclined to stay that way.

The natural healing force within each of us
is the greatest force in getting well.

HIPPOCRATES

This is happiness:
to be dissolved into something
complete and great.

WILLA CATHER

Your vision will become clear
only when you can look into your own heart.
Who looks outside, dreams;
who looks inside, awakes.

CARL JUNG

3

Healing is about something much larger than curing.

Your attentive presence to another can be useful, even therapeutic. But here we're adding the idea of *being healing* to the idea of *being present*. We're advocating not just any kind of presence, but a particular kind—*healing* presence.

What healing is not.

Healing is not the same as curing. It does not mean to apply a remedy that eliminates a person's disease or distress. Nor does healing involve fixing what may seem to be wrong in others' lives. This would assume there's something faulty in them or their situation. Nor is healing synonymous with making another person well. Many people imagine that's what a physician does by prescribing medication or performing a procedure, but that's not the case. Over 200 years ago, the French essayist Voltaire wrote: "The art of medicine consists of amusing the patient while nature cures the disease." Healing is not something you can *make* happen in someone else, no matter who you are, no matter what kind of training you have.

What healing is.

The true meaning of healing is revealed within the word itself. "Heal" comes from the same root as our word "whole." Healing suggests the idea of wholeness, and specifically any movement toward that wholeness. It refers to something that is already present and available in some form, something that is being drawn to become more complete in itself. It suggests a return to a state of original soundness. With that in mind, healing can take place in an arm that has been injured, a heart that has been broken, a life that has been shattered, or a relationship that has been damaged.

Seen in this light, healing is not something you can cause in another. You can be alert for healing potential and share this aware- ness as you see it arising. You can bring attention to what you already notice taking place deep within another, helping that person name it for himself, claim it for herself. You can foster those conditions that nurture any movement toward wholeness, whether those conditions are in you, the other person, people nearby, or the world around. You can affirm the authenticity of each human being—body, mind, heart and soul stretching into the fullness for which each of us is created.

What a healer is and does.

In her book *Kitchen Table Wisdom*, Rachel Naomi Remen describes how one of her patients defined what a healer is. It's someone, the patient said, who can see your movement toward wholeness more clearly than you're able to yourself at a given point in time. That's an accurate description of what may happen with healing presence. You are present for anything in the other that reaches out toward completeness. Each time you are aware of this impulse or movement, you can appreciate it, encourage it, and bless it. As a healer, however, you can do no more. And you don't *need* to do any more. Healing has a power and an intention all its own.

It moves with its own limitless energy, supplying its own intuitive wisdom.

When you accompany another in this way, any healing that begins to occur is not limited to the other. Naturally, you dare not do this for the purpose of promoting your own healing. It is *their* healing you always hold before you. But if you do this with *only* their healing as a possibility, you diminish the movement. For as you encourage their healing, you invite and honor your own, and the movement will circle again and again, extending the possibilities and promises of wholeness for you both.

Where healing comes from.

Science can explain the biology and psychology of healing. Medicine and therapy can optimize and sustain an environment for healing. But the ultimate source of healing lies beyond both human knowledge and human ability.

Healing is a sign of life's desire to refresh and renew itself. It is evidence that life has been infused with a vitality that allows for regeneration, sometimes even resurrection. Healing is an energy that pulses through all living matter, leading irresistibly toward wholeness. Even death does not exhaust it. Death is an essential part of the cycle of healing but is not its final word.

Ultimately, healing is rooted in the Source of life itself. It is the original act of creation taking place again and again, in bodies and minds, in people's stories and dreams, in their relationships and accomplishments. It is the same act that takes place each time you reach out to another in reverence and openness. And it is what happens each time the other responds.

The greatest thing in the world
is for one to know how to be oneself.

MICHEL DE MONTAIGNE

To reach something good it is useful to have gone astray,
and thus acquire experience.

TERESA OF AVILA

You can search the ten-fold universe
and not find a single being more worthy
of loving kindness than yourself.

BUDDHA

4

As you move toward being a healing presence, there's only one place to begin—with yourself.

It seems common sense to focus on the other person first. Who is she? What brought her to you? What is happening with him? What does he need?

But that's not the first step. Before getting curious about who someone else is, get curious about who *you* are. What is your personality style? How has your family history influenced who you are and how you act today? What significant life experiences have molded you, and how? What feelings do you commonly have, and when do you commonly have them? What are your important needs?

As you become more clear about who you are and why you do what you do, you will become more receptive to whomever you're with. Until then, while you may think you're seeing only them, in reality you'll still have yourself in the picture. A discomfort you feel with another might really have its root in you. An uneasy relationship with someone else, especially from early in your life, may be spilling over onto *this* relationship. Something unresolved within you may be showing its need for healing. These things occur frequently. The important thing is not that this happens but how you respond when it *does* happen. Are you willing to open and to become more curious about yourself as a first step toward becoming more present to those you accompany?

Open to your individuality.

You are, without question, unrepeatably unique. You may be hesitant, however, to claim your uniqueness, thinking other people are more "together" than you are. Yet it's precisely your individuality that's needed for healing presence. If you try to be present to another the way someone else would do it, you will leave behind part of yourself. You won't be able to fully connect with those you accompany because you won't be all there. The honoring of your uniqueness and theirs is what makes the connection between you work. When you claim and share your own individuality, you validate and encourage theirs.

Open to your humanness.

Being human is painful. Despite your best intentions, you may flounder. Despite your best efforts, you may fall short. Despite your best knowledge, you can be very wrong. Sometimes your human feelings are clear, while other times they're distressingly confusing. At times your feelings make perfect sense, and other times their source and energy is baffling. While you will have feelings you're proud of, sometimes it will hurt to admit you could be so jealous or petty or boastful. We are *all* that way sometimes. We are human. By opening to your humanness and accepting it, you allow others the safety of being human in your presence.

Open to your prejudices.

You will always have your biases, however much you wish you didn't, however conscientiously you try to overcome them. These personal judgments will automatically invade your relationships and will inevitably be sensed by others, despite your best intentions.

One way you can encourage your growth into healing presence is to become more aware of these prejudices—where they come from, what stimulates them today, what forms these biases take and how you tend to justify them. As you become more clear about your prejudices, you'll discover compassion for yourself and others, grounding your presence in authentic humility.

Open to your brokenness.

Like all people, you have caused injury to others or yourself. Like all people, you have been wounded, perhaps accidentally, perhaps intentionally. You may feel a sense of shame for the ways in which you are fragmented. You may want to hide those parts of you, as well as hide from them. Yet when you enter a relationship of healing presence, you are called out of hiding. You're called to see yourself and to be seen as you are. The more you can honestly own your vulnerability and brokenness, the more you can genuinely touch the healing potential that resides in both you and the other.

Healing presence asks you to be completely human and completely you. If you try to make yourself anything other than that, especially if you try to appear especially competent, especially sensitive, or especially "together," you create a distance between yourself and those you accompany. They are likely to feel they can't measure up to this false you. They will find it more difficult to be natural around you. Your healing presence will be less healing and less present.

Paradoxically, when you allow yourself to be with another as you naturally are, with all your frailties, you have already taken a sure step toward the wholeness that awaits you both.

Find a way, or make one.

LUCIUS SENECA

/3

If I had eight hours to chop down a tree,
I'd spend six sharpening my axe.

ABRAHAM LINCOLN

/3

What do we live for
if not to make the world less difficult
for each other?

MARY ANN EVANS

5

It helps to prepare a space if you're to be a healing presence.

Have you ever gone into another's home and felt especially comfortable and welcome there? Their hospitality put you at ease and gave you just the right amount of attention—not too little and not too much. The space they provided felt inviting and open. They seemed to enjoy having you there, just as you enjoyed being there.

Healing presence draws upon a similar sense of hospitality. You consciously create a space for another that feels welcoming, quieting and secure. There are several ways to invite this spaciousness.

Be adaptable.

Often the opportunity for healing presence is unanticipated. This possibility can be around every corner, occur at almost any time. The way to prepare a space for healing presence will vary from person to person, from place to place, and even from day to day. The variables are many.

You may go to the other person; he or she may come to you, or you may meet somewhere else. Your time together may be structured so you both know when it begins and ends, or your time may be informal and free-flowing. You may meet in private, or others may be nearby, perhaps even coming and going. Since healing presence can occur anywhere and at any time, flexibility and awareness are essential.

Clear the space between you.

It will help if there are few or, better, no barriers separating you. You want to relate to one another without the sense something is coming between you, unnecessarily restricting your communication. You can create a clearing and focusing effect simply by placing to one side any objects that are in the way. If possible, position yourself so anything immovable seems less obtrusive, for example, an article of furniture or a piece of medical equipment. Presuming you are in one another's physical presence, you ought to be able to see each other's face with ease.

Clear a space around you.

Certain elements in a space, even small elements, can be distracting. An opened magazine on your lap or a mass of papers in front of you may convey the message you're not completely available. Any visual clutter can make a room seem less than inviting. Perhaps you can help clear a space by drawing a curtain or closing a door, by turning down the radio or turning off the television. The more others sense they have space and freedom just to be who they are, the better.

Clear a space in time.

If you know when your time together will begin and end, make sure the other knows as well. Then do what you can to minimize distractions. Ensure that telephone calls are held or remain unan-swered. Silencing your pager, placing a note on the door to assure your privacy, or structuring other ways to protect this time emphasizes for you both the importance of the time you spend together.

Create an atmosphere of calm.

Calmness is always conducive to healing presence. Serenity serves as a constructive counterbalance to any agitation or unrest in the other person or in the surrounding environment. Because nurturing such an atmosphere may be easier if the other enters your space, it may help to suggest they come to you, if you have that option.

Through the subtle clearing you do and the thoughtful preparations you make, you give others the message that you have created room for them. There is space to spread out and share whatever they're experiencing. Regardless of the circumstances, it's good to remember you can always attend in some way to whatever space and time you share, even if it's no more than just turning your backs to something distracting or drawing closer so you can create a circle of quiet. One ingredient of being an effective healing presence is to recognize that whatever control you *do* have is enough. The smallest change in any environment can add quality, privacy and peace.

The only gift is a portion of thyself.

RALPH WALDO EMERSON

Be at peace with yourself first
and then you will be able
to bring peace to others.

THOMAS À KEMPIS

We can make our minds so like still water
that beings gather about us to see their own images,
and so live for a moment with a clearer,
perhaps even with a fiercer life
because of our silence.

WILLIAM BUTLER YEATS

6

The most important space you prepare is not around you but within you.

However conscientious you are about creating open, soothing space in the environment around you, it's even more important to create a similar space inside. When people sense you've made room for them within you, they are more likely to open up, to feel freer to be who they are, to claim their own healing potential. If you have prepared space internally for them, they will sense it. And if you have not, they will sense that too.

Create a stress-free zone inside.

A *completely* stress-free zone may be asking a bit much, given the nature of your work and the structures and strains you encounter each day. Stresses are real and can be considerable. So perhaps you can perform a simple exercise of naming for yourself each significant stress you feel one by one, then laying each aside for a given period of time—for the coming hour, during the next appointment, or through the rest of your workday. Maybe you can put a little psychological distance or spiritual perspective between yourself and these stresses, even if it is a small distance. Some form of physical exercise may help to do this. So can quiet meditation or prayer. Do you ever ask for prayer from others? This can help too.

Build a buffer between encounters.

Another way you can clear yourself is to let go of what was happening just prior to this time you have together. If you are moving from one person to the next, try intentionally leaving thoughts of the previous meeting behind, knowing you'll pick them up again. If you've been engaged in something that brought out strong feelings in you, try compartmentalizing those feelings temporarily so they don't disrupt your present encounter. Perhaps you can sit quietly for a few moments, write a quick entry in your journal, or hold a short conversation with a friend or colleague as a way of bringing closure to your previous exchange and centering yourself in readiness for the next.

If you don't have much time to prepare, perhaps you can simply stand for a moment and take a deep breath or two. Breathing slowly, you can recall your purpose and your intention to be present. Breathing steadily, you can tap into an energy that's deep within you, an energy you feel around you. Some people like to form "arrow prayers" of just a few words, such as "Help me hold this person in Your light," or "May I be with them as they need," or "May this be for the greater good of all."

Clear a space within, even when you're on the run.

You may not have the luxury of being able to prepare yourself as you would like. The telephone may ring, the door may open, or your name may be called and suddenly you're swept into a flow of ongoing requests and needs whether or not you feel ready for them. Remember to breathe evenly. With each inhalation, visualize an area being cleared away within you, little by little. Another option is to suggest the two of you pause for a moment in silence before you begin your time together.

Clear yourself of preoccupation.

With healing presence, it's always best simply to be who you are—authentically yourself. At the same time, it's also important to keep the preoccupations and superficialities of your life at bay. Your intention is to be present for the other person. How do you attend in this way? By speaking less rather than more. By calling yourself back to the person you're with each time you get caught up in your own thoughts. By talking about yourself and your own experiences rarely and only if such sharing will benefit the other. By seeing to it you have your own times, places, and people where healing presence is focused upon you. And by refraining from attempting to impose control over what happens as you accompany another. Unless you stay alert, it can be tempting to allow the intention to focus on the other to include focus on yourself.

Clear away your expectations.

Whomever you're accompanying will have their individual modes of relating and their natural ways of healing. Their movement toward wholeness may be slower than yours. Or faster. Their growth may take an entirely different route than any you have taken or witnessed. Some people move toward healing by working hard at it. Others do the opposite and relax into it. They may move toward self-understanding by talking, writing, praying, or being in silence.

By noticing and releasing any rigid expectations about what will happen in your time together, as well as what will happen after, you help clear the way for others to do what is theirs alone to do. You also help yourself do what is *yours* alone to do—to prepare a place within.

We are all one.

Respect depends on reciprocity.

AFRICAN PROVERB

In every person there is royalty.
Address the royalty and royalty will respond.

SCANDINAVIAN PROVERB

I reckon there's as much human nature
in some folks as there is in others, if not more.

EDWARD NOYES WESTCOTT

7

That other person is your equal in every way that really matters.

Both you and the person you're accompanying are unique, immersed in different life circumstances and roles. If you're the nurse or physician in a caregiving relationship, you have specialized knowledge and training that exceeds that of the patient. The same is true if you're a counselor, social worker, teacher, or clergyperson. If you're the parent of an underage child, one of you has more say than the other. But where healing presence is concerned, whoever you are, you're equal—equally human, equally created, equally capable, equally loved.

An inequality, however, may exist in any situation and relationship that invites healing presence. In our society, for example, illness often connotes that sick people are somehow less—less than they used to be, less than they could be. This is true whether the illness is physical, mental, or spiritual, whether the condition is temporary or long-standing.

Those physically ill or incapacitated are likely to be situated in a bed, chair or wheelchair. This means they have to look up as you approach, and it encourages you to look down upon them. Clothing provided for ill people, especially any institutional dress, may further denote this "less than" quality, suggesting less power, less authority, less normalcy in life. Even the word "patient" carries the not-so-subtle hint that such a person is supposed to behave less energetically, more passively. People with terminal illness may be looked upon as being less than fully alive, even though life may be surging through them with uncommon intensity and urgency.

Whether the other person is in a healthcare setting, at home, or anywhere else, what can you do to communicate clearly your equality?

Honor the other's significance.

When you honor others, you show regard for them. That is how people you accompany deserve to be treated—with respect and reverence. They are infinitely worthy. Their life experiences are significant. Whoever they are, in one way or another they have been acquainted with adversity and pain; they have experienced satisfaction and joy. As writer Gustave Flaubert noted, "Every person's life is worth a novel." In truth, every person's life is worth far more than a novel.

If your role is professional, you can honor the significance of others by learning, using, and remembering each person's name. You can address them in the way they prefer. Will it be "Mr.," "Mrs.," or "Ms."? Will they offer you their first name or a nickname? It's theirs to decide. Addressing someone as "sweetie" or "honey" or some other term of affection when you haven't known them by that name before can be received as demeaning. Those whom you accompany will experience your respect by the way you look at them and listen to them, by the manner in which you touch them, by the tone in which you speak to them—all ways in which you can honor that which is unique and precious in each one.

Honor their natural healing ability.

All people have within them the God-given potential to develop, expand, and become fully alive. Every person comes into the world possessing a natural desire to be whole. So you can relax and rest in the knowledge that the other's progress in healing is not your responsibility. You can help them claim and honor their own healing potential, however it might arise or extend. If they have not been aware of this capacity, you can help them see it and claim it. If they have forgotten this capacity, you can encourage them in remembering it. If they have lost trust in that capacity, you can communicate by your presence and example that it *is* worth trusting again.

Honor their sacred humanity.

Walt Whitman once wrote: "If anything is sacred, the human body is." He might just as easily have written that if anything is sacred, the human face is. The human life. The human spirit.

Clearly, human life, given its baffling complexity, did not just inadvertently happen. It was somehow guided into being, somehow created. Deep within what is mortal lies something immortal. When you approach another with this awareness, you find yourself face-to-face with a sense of sacred mystery. The face of the Divine in you recognizes the face of the Divine in the other person. When you stand before one another in this way, you are on holy ground.

Silence is healing for all ailments.

HEBREW PROVERB

⌒3

It takes two to speak the truth—
one to speak, and another to hear.

HENRY DAVID THOREAU

⌒3

When a companion's heart of itself overflows,
the best one can do is do nothing.

HERMAN MELVILLE

8

Your healing presence can take many forms.

You cannot *do* healing presence—you *become* healing presence, expressing it gently yet firmly in various ways. Your ways will not be someone else's, even though you may share the same occupation, or be engaged in similar caregiving as a volunteer or family member. Your healing presence will shift and extend as you gather experience and age. It will take on different expressions in response to the one you're with.

Listening. Perhaps you've heard this popular advice: "There are three things you can do to help someone. The first is to listen. The second is to listen. The third is to listen some more." When you listen to others, you value them. You quietly and clearly communicate that you care. Real listening, the kind that occurs at a level well beyond the polite professional and social norm, requires concentration, focus and effort. When you listen in this way, the other will feel affirmed and validated, perhaps freed and empowered.

Holding. You can hold others mentally as you focus your thoughts on them throughout the day. You can hold them spiritually as you make them a part of your daily disciplines, or as you reach out to them soul-to-soul. You may physically hold the other person by taking a hand, touching an arm or shoulder, or perhaps even offering an embrace. Your sensitivity is crucial here. Some people aren't ready or willing to be touched. Ask them first. Or extend your touch in such a way they can easily and comfortably withdraw if they wish.

Talking. Healing presence involves very little speaking for the one who is simply present. "What should I say?" is the most common question for someone who's new at this, yet what you say will have far less impact than how you listen. Still, it often helps to speak. You can respond honestly to their questions, including saying "I don't know" if that's the case. You don't *have* to know. Despite their questions, others don't *expect* you to know. Your presence itself validates their feelings, their situation, their process. Occasionally, you might reveal parts of yourself and your own story. Always the purpose of *your* talk is to invite *their* talk.

Being silent. Sitting in silence with others can be deeply healing. You're not waiting for their next words. You're simply going deeply into the moment together, united by this quiet you share. As you open to it, you can listen for what this rich silence is saying, to each of you and to both of you.

Being still. Quieting your body helps to keep focus on them. You do this by looking directly at them rather than all around them, by sitting still rather than fidgeting, by being aware of any nervous habits you have that might be distracting.

Being in your body. As you're with another, you can bring attention to your entire physical being. What is your whole body telling you? What sensations do you have in your chest, your throat, your neck? What do your insides tell you? Developing a reliable connection with your body opens intuitive channels for receiving valuable information well beyond what you can pick up with your eyes and ears.

Coming home to yourself. It is essential to be naturally yourself with others. You're not a role —you're you. So follow your instincts. Trust your intuition. The more you're at home with yourself, the more the other is also invited and drawn naturally to a centered place.

Being receptive. As you still yourself in the other's presence, you wait patiently and open-mindedly for what will come, without trying to control the results. You accept willingly what the other has to say. You embrace freely and gratefully what this experience offers.

Other options abound. You can deepen your healing presence by slowing down, by doing only one thing at a time, by reminding yourself regularly to come back to the present moment. You can encourage healing presence by being appreciative, forgiving, humble, kind.

Don't expect too much of yourself. If you do, you'll be concentrating so much on process that you'll miss the intimacy of the moment. Choose the forms that are an authentic expression for you. How will you know? By experimenting. By following your curiosity. By trusting your sixth sense. By being true to your personal style. By praying for guidance.

Again, remember we all have our own unique way of being a healing presence. The more you stay true to your own natural style, the more you'll be grounded in the essence of healing presence itself.

All things are possible
to one who believes.

BERNARD OF CLAIRVAUX

∕ℨ

The art of being wise
is the art of knowing what to overlook.

WILLIAM JAMES

∕ℨ

To be what we are,
and to become what we are capable of becoming,
is the only end of life.

ROBERT LOUIS STEVENSON

9

One of the most powerful things you can do for someone as a healing presence is simply believe.

"My strength is gone. I wonder if it will return."

"I feel stuck in life. I can't go backward, and it seems impossible to go forward."

"The odds are stacked hopelessly against me. I may as well give up."

It's not uncommon to hear such words from those who are in need of healing. A long series of struggles may have drained both energy and confidence. Life may seem less dependable than it once was. Hope for anything better may be fading fast or even long gone. And when hope recedes, so does the capacity to move toward healing and wholeness. That's where your presence is invited.

What can you do when people don't believe in themselves, when they doubt the possibilities? *You* can choose to believe, even if they don't. You believe whether or not you see evidence of their capacity to move in that direction. That doesn't matter—you remain steadfast in your conviction.

"Holding certainty" is another way of describing this act of believing. This is not about persuading others to think or act in a different way. Nor is it about encouraging them to become optimistic or hopeful. Holding certainty simply means you consciously hold a vision of the potential for wholeness that exists. While you have no illusion that the way ahead will be easy or clear, you carry a strong conviction that something healing, something life-giving, can occur.

Holding certainty for someone, you may do things like this:

You say: "I believe you'll make it through this situation," and you really do believe it.

You say: "I don't know exactly where this is heading, but I feel confident you're discovering your way." Then you staunchly maintain that confidence on their behalf.

You may say little, realizing it's too early to say more. Nonetheless, you communicate certainty with your face, eyes, and tone of voice.

When you truly see the other as creative, capable, and possessing possibility, the certainty communicates itself effortlessly.

If the other person lacks this certainty, how can you maintain your own belief?

Recall what you already know.

There is deep potential for healing in all of life. You've witnessed it. You've experienced growth and positive, enduring change within yourself. You've seen healing take place in other individuals, in families, in relationships. You've watched it take form in nature. You trust this healing because not only is it real—it is perpetual.

Hold an image of whomever is in your care.

You can visualize others tapping into their own potential and moving toward what provides them with meaning. This is not an image of your expectation for them. Rather, it is a vision of wholeness you're maintaining that can help activate, sooner or later, the possibility that is always there.

Live out the reality of the other's separateness.
This other person is a completely separate individual who is not
only free to make his or her own decisions but is the one who *must*
make those decisions. You maintain your sure knowledge that they
are the only ones who, in fact, can ultimately choose what's right for
them. You trust them to do that by encouraging their absolute freedom
to change and grow.

Serve as a consultant to the other's process.
When it seems appropriate, you can offer back to them what
you see—your understanding of their situation in a larger frame of
reference. When a decision must be made, you can be a consultant,
providing insight, objective reasoning, and support, if that's what
they wish. From your training and life experiences, you can lift up
any choices you know to be available. What resources are on hand?
Who else might be consulted? Where might more information be
found? Offer this input in such a way that it can be easily amended,
accepted, or rejected altogether. Whatever their decisions, you stand
for their movement toward conscious choice-making.

Holding certainty is one of the most profound ways you can be a
healing presence. With your words, inflection, body language, faith,
and overall approach, you affirm the capacity we all have to heal
and grow, including particularly that one person you're presently
accompanying.

Mistrust your zeal for doing good to others.

ABBÉ HUVELIN

/3

If I knew a man was coming to my house
with the conscious design of doing me good,
I should run for my life.

HENRY DAVID THOREAU

/3

It brings me comfort and encouragement
to have companions in whatever happens.

DIO CHRYSOSTOM

/3

The greatest good you can do for another
is not just to share your riches,
but reveal to them their own.

BENJAMIN DISRAELI

10

Healing presence is most effective when it is least active.

Your desire to help flows out of your best intentions. You witness what is happening to others, and you want to make their situation a little easier or better. You may have been through a similar experience yourself. Perhaps you've gained wisdom from others. You may be someone who has been a natural caregiver for as long as you can remember. Or your caregiving may be a recent role, whether you wanted it or not. Perhaps you've had professional training, so when you see someone in pain or fear or grief, you've been prepared to do something about it.

It's possible, however, that your good intentions and natural inclinations may limit your healing presence.

Sometimes helping isn't helpful.

There's a common idea that helping means doing something for someone else, and the more you do, the better helper you are. This isn't necessarily so. When you do for others what they could do on their own, or wish to attempt on their own, you potentially take away their authority and control. You diminish the satisfaction they may feel in their own accomplishments, as well as the knowledge they might gain or any strength they might build from their experience or situation.

Trying to reduce others' psychological or spiritual anguish, to diminish their apparent pain, is also inappropriate. To interfere in this way despite all good intention will discourage or delay the healing process, a process that often involves intense feeling. And the unfortunate message that is often conveyed is that they don't have the resources or the competence to feel or to learn on their own.

Sometimes helping isn't possible.

The other may refuse your helping, no matter how much help you think you have to give. And some forms of help are unseemly or impossible. You cannot take on or take away others' discomfort or pain—it's theirs alone. You cannot handle or change their feelings— that's beyond your ability. Nor can you manage their healing for them, since every person must heal for herself or himself, however difficult that may be, however long it takes.

Sometimes the most effective helping doesn't look that way.

Healing presence will look less like helping than you might anticipate. You've probably heard this reversal of a popular expression: "Don't just do something—stand there!" Any help that you are as a healing presence follows the same philosophy: Don't just do something—sit there! Don't just rush to say something—hush there! Don't hurry to make things better—just listen, support, allow.

Your helping may take the form of reflecting back in your own words what you are hearing. "This is what I am sensing," you might say as you begin. Using as few words and as much clarity as possible, you share your perception. Then you hush and listen some more.

The help of healing presence is like pulling alongside.

The help of healing presence looks like this: visualize one person coming up beside another who's walking along and falling in step beside that person. In such a situation, what is it that helps?

You help when you walk with them, matching your pace to theirs. You help when you walk in the direction they're moving, even if it seems directionless, rather than leading them the way you want to go. You help when you walk close enough that you can hear and be heard with ease, but you don't walk so closely that they feel crowded. Sometimes you look at them and sometimes you don't, but either way, they know beyond a doubt they're being seen.

Even if those you accompany are agitated or troubled, you consciously and lovingly choose not to be. Even if they are excited or speak rapidly, you communicate in your own natural rhythm and voice. You take time in responding, waiting for words to come, or not to come. This waiting can be an invitation for others to do their own waiting, if they wish. You can help by resting in your own quiet center as you move along together. Without speaking a word about it, you're saying: "You too have this same quiet center in you."

When you practice healing presence, the effect is subtle. You don't appear to be doing very much, and the other doesn't necessarily appear to be receiving a great deal. Yet as you stay attuned, something takes place. Maybe you see the other relax a little and breathe more freely. Maybe they open up and speak more honestly. Perhaps they share a feeling, have an insight, lighten a little. You may have little idea of anything changing, yet the other can be shifting profoundly.

This movement in others will flow from your caring self-restraint as a helper. You carefully and lovingly contribute less, so that more can take place in them.

Be near me when my light is low.

ALFRED, LORD TENNYSON

♪

Love is all we have,
the only way each can help the other.

EURIPIDES

♪

Sometimes it is more important to discover
what one cannot do than what one can do.

LIN YUTANG

♪

We must, strictly speaking, at every moment
give each other up and let each other go
and not hold each other back.

RAINER MARIA RILKE

11

Healing presence involves being connected while maintaining separateness.

Healing presence takes place only within relationship. The relationship may be very close—your spouse or partner, a dear relative, an intimate friend. Just as easily, this relationship may be more casual—a colleague, a patient, an acquaintance, a member of your congregation. Whatever the relationship, healing presence calls for both intimacy and separation.

Show your willingness to connect.

Others may question whether you're really interested in being with them. They may wonder if you're ready to accept what they have to lay before you. Perhaps they have sought connection with someone before and found that person to be hesitant or uncomfortable with them. Perhaps they remember how *they* have responded when the roles were reversed, how *they* hesitated, how *they* steered clear, how *they* were fearful. They may presume this is what usually goes on with all people, including you.

Others may have misconceptions about what it's like for you to be a healing presence. They may presume you will come away from your time together feeling upset or depressed. They may feel they're imposing on you terribly, when you don't feel that way at all. So it's up to you to demonstrate your openness to being with the other and your willingness to draw closer.

Offer your empathy.

Empathy is the conscious and intuitive attempt to know without judgment and as accurately as possible what the other person is experiencing. This is different from sympathy, when you respond by matching others on a feeling level. Empathy imparts greater understanding and creates more depth between you, as well as a larger sense of both equality and safety for the other.

To empathize, you recall within yourself a time when you felt even a particle or thread of what another person now seems to feel. With that beginning, you continue to listen carefully with your heart, mind, and soul, coming as close as you can to appreciating what his or her experience is like. You don't try to duplicate it within you— you just stay with it, fathoming it as well as you can.

Offer unconditional positive regard.

When you meet others in the moment, accepting them exactly as they are, you prepare the way for them to just be, without pretension and without excuse. You relate to them out of the belief they're doing the best they can at this time. You see them as children of God, just as you are, and more than that, as imperfect children, also as you are.

The more you learn to do this, the better you become at offering what psychologist Carl Rogers called "unconditional positive regard." Buddhists name this "offering loving-kindness." Christians describe it as "loving your neighbor as yourself." Whatever you choose to call it, it means you relate to others in a way that's gentle, non-judging and respectful.

Guarantee your closeness by keeping some space between you.

Odd as it may seem, the way you draw close to others through your healing presence is by making sure you stay a certain distance apart. It will be your responsibility, more than theirs, to maintain this space.

Sometimes what's going on in another's life may touch you deeply—so deeply it can feel overwhelming. For example, if the other is dying, you may find it painful to be close by, to witness all that is happening. It's likely to evoke feelings about your own mortality and the mortality of those you love. Something similar can happen if the other person's situation involves a serious illness, a trauma, a loss, or some other distressing experience. Find a way to resolve your reactions outside this relationship; otherwise, you'll limit your capacity for presence with both this person and others. They'll sense you feel frightened or inundated and pull back, to protect you or themselves or both of you.

Keeping some space between you will help to prevent your getting too intertwined with others. Stay clear about your respective roles. Part of healing involves others feeling their own feelings, listening to their own hearts, making their own decisions, living their own lives. Part of healing presence involves your doing the same thing, but separately. Maintaining this space between you allows you to be more objective, to view a wider perspective.

So paradoxically, healing presence is equally a matter of drawing together and staying apart. One way you can maintain your closeness is to protect your separateness.

As long as you derive inner help
and comfort from anything,
keep it.

MAHATMA GANDHI

A person too busy to take care of one's own health
is like a mechanic too busy to take care of one's own tools.

SPANISH PROVERB

This is one of the smaller planets
and people cannot work in the same directions
and care for each other
without meeting occasionally.

MARY BRECKENRIDGE

12

You cannot be a healing presence entirely on your own. You need support and nurture.

While you're being wholly present with another person, in one sense you are very much on your own. No one else can be there in your place. No one else can do your listening for you or understand for you. In another sense, however, healing presence is infinitely broader in scope than what you do with others, and you're far from alone. Support and nurture are continually available from many sources.

Sometimes you'll invite or enable this support, and other times it will simply be there when you need it. Sometimes you'll intuitively know what will encourage healing presence for you, and other times it will come to you as pure gift and grace. Since you are a whole person and healing presence is a holistic endeavor, any nurturing must be holistic too. It must involve all that is you: body, heart, soul, and mind.

Nurture your body.

Your body is the most obvious part of you. Yet how obvious to you are its needs? Do you regularly pay attention to what your body asks for? Do you follow through and do what's best for it? Do you appreciate your body?

Physically, are you merely reactive to what your body tells you about its condition? Or do you invite and encourage health rather than just attend to illness? This is a very real project that takes time and effort and sometimes money. But there are resources and people to assist. Find them. Join the Y. Do yoga. Eat nutritiously. Get rest. Drink water, lots of it. Take vitamins. Have a massage. Find a walking partner. Jog. Rollerblade. Swim. Call yourself to be in your body and make your body a good home for your self. Be grateful for it.

Nurture your heart.

It's important to be able to tell your truth to someone. Maybe it's your spouse or life partner, a good friend or close relative. It's a relief to pick up the phone or begin an email or knock on a door and say to someone who appreciates you, "I'm a mess at the moment," and know she or he will listen and understand—and be just as supportive if you say, "Life is good! Today I'm celebrating!"

Perhaps it will be valuable to spend time with a professional who can help you sort out some of your own inner conflicts. Open up to others like yourself who serve in healing. Keep a journal. Read poetry. Draw. Paint. Garden. Photograph. Throw a party. Make music. Laugh often and cry well. In those ways that suit you best, stay close to the urgings of your heart.

Nurture your soul.

There are people willing to sit with you and help you discover the voice of God within. They're called spiritual directors or companions. Consider talking with one. Meet with a prayer partner. Read devotional materials. Meditate on sacred texts. Pray throughout your day. Worship. Attend a workshop at a spiritual growth center. Take time for a silent retreat. Contemplate as you sit and look at an object of beauty.

Contemplate as you walk, as you arrange flowers, as you do the dishes. Let your self relax and let your soul be at peace.

Nurture your mind.

If you're like many, you feel overly busy already. Yet it is essential to keep expanding both your mind and your imagination. The possibilities are endless. Consider enrolling in a class or continuing education course. Pursue a field in which you're interested. Read the latest books. Read the earliest books. Listen to audiobooks. Subscribe to journals. Attend lectures. Question. Think. Discuss. Decide.

True healing presence occurs at a profound level of consciousness—one that most of us do not maintain very long on a day-to-day basis. The only way to grow into this consciousness and hold it for any length of time is to be intentional about seeking it and discplined about finding ways to sustain it. Discover your particular ways of nourishing and supporting your sensitivity and your authenticity.

Deep experience is never peaceful.

HENRY JAMES

❧

Where there is love, there is pain.

ENGLISH PROVERB

❧

The one who wants a rose
must respect the thorn.

PERSIAN PROVERB

❧

When the heart weeps for what it has lost,
the soul rejoices for what it has found.

SUFI PROVERB

13

Healing presence can bring considerable joy as well as its share of discomfort.

Joy is one of the signs of healing presence. Nevertheless, healing presence will not always be joyful, for sadness and pain are natural to wholeness.

There is joy enough to go around.

Whatever is happening in the other's life, you can take joy in who this person is—marvelously created, interestingly molded. You can take pleasure in the brighter aspects of other people's stories— perhaps how they found their way where there wasn't a clear path, how they discovered themselves when they felt completely lost. You can experience heartfelt satisfaction with people as they heal their way into life and perhaps even into death, as they go all the way through their sorrow to find their deep gladness on the other side.

You can also take joy in your own situation—you are willing to serve, to be present in whatever ways are genuinely yours. You can find fulfillment in the relationship that develops between you, for however long it lasts. You can feel gratified at what you experience together, including the sense of pleasant surprise when the one you started to help suddenly begins to help you as you discover more about yourself and about life. You can know the joy of realizing you're *each* becoming more whole as a result of what takes place between you.

There is even laughter to be heard.

Sometimes you'll experience the kind of joy that's downright funny. Have you ever tried hard not to laugh during a worship service or in some other situation where such behavior would seem inappropriate, barely able contain yourself? Or have you ever been with another when things were just so awful you both spontaneously started to giggle? Or have you ever been with someone as you grieved a significant loss and found yourselves crying, and later laughing, before crying again?

Healing presence is frequently humorous in a similar way. You may develop inside jokes with one another as you go along. You may laugh at one another's innocent foibles. You may experience delightful serendipities as a problem is suddenly overcome or a fear unexpectedly dissipates, as grace makes its grand appearance or as courage quietly resumes its place within. Whether your response is to smile or giggle or laugh, you are present to joy.

There will also be the other: discomfort, even sadness.

If you presume those you accompany will move quickly and surely toward some ideal of wholeness, you will find yourself frustrated. They may not seem to move in a direction like that at all. Or they may apparently move so slowly and sporadically in the direction they've chosen that it becomes tiring or trying to you. Healing presence may take more time, more effort, and more understanding than you originally imagined.

You will inevitably encounter periods when you'll feel uncomfortably filled up with all the difficulties—the sadness, the suffering, the grief. Alternatively, you may at times feel completely emptied out.

You may sense your capacity to feel deeply about *anything* is diminished. You may feel numb.

From time to time, you will also experience another dynamic. Some aspect of what's happening to the other person will activate something uncomfortable or painful in you. It may resurrect memories you had hoped to forget. It may stir up emotions you've kept well contained. There's nothing unusual or wrong with these responses on your part. They're simply signs pointing to those areas within you that are asking for attention, illumination, and perhaps some healing.

You may find you just don't "click" with whomever you're with. They may be loud when you're used to quiet. They may be quiet when you wished they would speak more. They may appear outwardly cantankerous or inwardly sullen. They may expect more from you than you're able to offer. Whatever the discomforts, it's important to be aware of them, name them to yourself, and prayerfully try to understand what's going on, both within the other person and within yourself.

Another pain you're likely to experience is the pain of perceived failure. You're going to make mistakes. You'll say the wrong things. You'll miss an important clue. You'll let the other person down without even knowing it. Your errors will be as unavoidable as the regret that follows them. So you'll need to be fluent in forgiveness, for yourself as well as for others.

One truth about healing presence is that the depth to which you can go within yourself corresponds directly to the depth at which you can connect intimately with another. This holds true for all you experience—the pain *and* the joy.

If you want to lift yourself up,
lift up someone else.

BOOKER T. WASHINGTON

/3

We are rich only through what we give,
and poor only through what we refuse.

ANNIE-SOPHIE SWETCHINE

/3

You will find that the mere resolve not to be useless,
and the honest desire to help other people,
will, in the quickest and delicatest ways,
improve yourself.

JOHN RUSKIN

14

As a healing presence, you won't receive as much as you give. You're likely to receive even more.

Another paradox is evident through your healing presence. You give to others what may not seem like much but is really an abundance. Then those others often give something in return, which also may not seem like much but is really more than enough. Add together what you each have to give, and there will be an overflow.

What might you personally receive?

You'll find yourself living more of your moments, and living them more fully.

When you stay in the present moment with others as much as you're able, you go about your days with an increased awareness that enriches *your* life too. You see more, and whatever you see, you see more clearly. You're more attuned to *all* your senses, more conscious of *all* parts of your body, more aware of *all* your relationships with everyone and everything. You squander less of your time because you're aware it's so precious. You lay claim to more of your passing days because you live them thoroughly and use them well. And you stay clear that you can and must occasionally gloriously, joyfully and gratefully fritter a day away.

You'll uncover more of your genuine self.

As you make yourself more naturally available to others, you become increasingly available to yourself. You hide less—both from you and from them. You speak truthfully, and your truthfulness is literally life-giving. As a result, you become more and more authentically yourself—more transparent. People respond positively when your inward depth is reflected outwardly. The more this happens, the more others respond in a similar fashion. It starts a circle of increasing transparency that goes on and on.

You'll forge some wonderful relationships.

As you open to others, they are likely to open to you, gifting you with meaningful experiences of honesty, insight and growth. They'll share with you their histories, their longings, their dreams— in other words, they will share the essence of who they are. You'll not soon forget their stories. Perhaps you'll never forget what they have given you. As all this takes place, thanksgiving will flow in both directions.

You'll receive the gift of a grateful heart.

Few experiences are more gratifying than knowing you have been present as another moved toward wholeness. You may hear someone say, "You made all the difference," and while you realize the credit lies largely beyond you, you're humbly pleased to accept the gift of your limited role. For ultimately, healing presence is energy that is channeled *through* you, and you are only the vessel. Yet what a privilege to be such a vessel!

You'll be bestowed some of life's most important lessons.

This motto was inscribed above the doorways of ancient European hospices: "The dying become our teachers." Something similar is at work here: Those whom you companion become the bearers of your lessons. As you draw close to others and wait with them, you'll learn and relearn that small kindnesses can address large needs and have lasting impact. As you offer witness and hold certainty for others, you'll be taught again and again that while pain is universal, with time and support, with gentleness and prayer, it can also lead to healing and be potently life-giving.

Every person you accompany will have a life lesson to teach you. You'll be shown that fear and struggle can become agents for growth. Death and grief can become seeds for new life. Love can overcome all barriers separating heaven and earth. You'll discover this because you'll be experiencing it. You'll know this because you'll not just see it—you'll live it.

By remaining at the heart of healing presence, you'll learn that there is no clear distinction between the one who gives and the one who receives—it is all one dynamic flow. You'll comprehend in a way you have not before that all of us stand in the never-ending cycle of creation—the cycle of life and death and new life emerging out of death. Within this cycle, the difficult and painful life experiences— even the most terrible ones—can herald transformation.

As for me, I know nothing else but miracles.

WALT WHITMAN

/3

O seekers, remember, all distances are traversed
by those who yearn to be near the source of their being.

KABIR

/3

After you had taken your leave,
I found God's footprints on my floor.

RABINDRANATH TAGORE

/3

Certain thoughts are prayers.
There are certain moments when,
whatever the attitude of the body,
the soul is on its knees.

VICTOR HUGO

15

Healing presence is filled with sacredness.

Healing presence is everything life itself is: messy and mysterious, exasperating and exhilarating, wearying and wonderful.

That's what makes it so sacred.

The sacred reveals itself everywhere.

Meister Eckhart, the 13th Century German mystic, once wrote: "Suppose someone in hiding stirs, showing their whereabouts there. God does the same. No one could have found God—God gave Himself away."

Whatever name or description you ascribe to the Divine, this truth remains: The sacred can be less than visible in the everyday world, until it comes out of hiding. Truly, that which is sacred has been present all along, but often you haven't been looking for it. From time to time you catch glimmers or glimpses, but so much of the time, like everyone, you become captive to your daily routines, the familiar sights, your customary thoughts.

Beneath and throughout those common routines, however, is a deeper truth: The sacred reveals itself in the earthy and the earthly, in what is considered most ordinary. In fact, that's the only place that holiness can reveal itself if our very human and earthly eyes are to see it.

Discipline heightens awareness of the sacred.

Sometimes we forget the sacred. Other times we remember to look but cannot see. That's when everyday practices can bring you back to the sacred again. Worship within community can remind you. Ritual, music, and scripture can open the eye of the heart. Prayer, spoken or silent, can focus and heighten spiritual awareness. Any intentional practice that explores your inner being can also be a discipline strengthening your connection to the sacred—developing a gift of artistic expression, committing to some form of justice in action, planting a garden, walking in the woods.

Whether you practice this discipline alone or with others, frequently or only rarely, you are continually drawn toward what it can offer. By remaining faithful to your practice, even when it sometimes feels empty, you are constantly reminded of those sacred connections. In time, you will experience the truth as captured by the Jewish theologian, Abraham Heschel: "Just to be is a blessing. Just to live is holy."

Life experiences that stretch you create natural openings to the sacred.

When someone you love becomes mortally ill, life's preciousness is suddenly and dramatically made tangible and real. When someone you love dies or abandons you, you're confronted with issues of meaning and purpose—life's meaning and your purpose. The birth of a child or the fulfillment of a dream can awaken you to both the grace and the mystery lying at life's center. The experience of being seen and accepted, being loved, and being forgiven will also do this.

Many opportunities for healing presence grow out of times exactly like these, when you experience the utter fullness of your humanity and the stunning blessing of life on earth.

Healing presence is essentially a spiritual discipline in itself.

As you begin, you may think of healing presence primarily as something you do for someone else. Eventually, however, you'll realize that healing presence has become an integral and significant part of your own spiritual development. As you choose to keep opening yourself to this discipline, even when it's difficult, even when you feel yourself rebelling, you necessarily mature spiritually. As you repeatedly ask yourself, "How can I be a healing presence in this particular situation?", you expand your horizons and you make new and fruitful connections with all dimensions of life, especially life's sacred foundation. The more you are a healing presence in the midst of everyday events, the more you come to appreciate that the common ground on which you stand with another is pulsing with all that is divine. You realize that holiness is at work as you consciously and compassionately accompany others. Then sometimes when you least expect it, a sense of awe overwhelms you—awe, perhaps strong assurance, or waves of gratitude, or an immense sense of peace.

You cannot make any of this happen. You can only welcome it as it unfolds, revealing itself and making its presence known. It is The Sacred.

If you do not expect the unexpected you will not find it.
for it is not to be reached by search or trail.

HERACLITUS

ß

And we are put on earth a little space
that we might learn to bear the beams of love.

WILLIAM BLAKE

ß

All shall be well, and all shall be well,
and all manner of things shall be well.

JULIAN OF NORWICH

And now,
what does healing presence invite?

As people experience healing presence, they change. This
shift may be subtle or dramatic. They're likely to open more—to
themselves, to others, to the world, to the amazing mystery of life
itself. Sensing another's belief in them, and seeing that belief
reflected in life around them, they can begin to develop in completely
unexpected ways, and to move in directions they have not gone before.
Or perhaps they will return to their original path, but with new spirit,
new vision, new hope. As they encounter the inevitable pains and
diminishments that life will present, they can begin to understand that
such adversities can be experienced as more than adversities—they can
be known as opportunities for growth, as avenues for moving toward
wholeness.

Your authenticity and the compassion in your presence will fan
out generously around you, always returning to envelop you again
and again. As you become less driven by your own concerns and less
given to your own needs, and as you forsake your need to help, you'll
become a more mature and helpful companion. As you give yourself
daily, even hourly, to what healing kindles within you, you'll relinquish
more of your narrow and willful demands and claims on life. As you
do so, you'll find joy and abundance dancing naturally in their stead,
filling more and more of your passing moments.

Such changes are not yours to own or to keep for yourself—they are meant to ripple out in all directions, touching family, friends, colleagues, patients, clients, anyone with whom you come into contact. Healing spirals, issuing its invitation to all others—those who are around you, those who are beyond you. And because this is such a life-giving force, others *will* respond, others *will* be present, others *will* heal.

This force, this energy is nothing less than transformative. As former, restricting ways of relating are surrendered, an inner freedom and an expanding love are born. This transformation takes place right before your eyes, through commonplace happenings, in everyday relationships, in all sorts of families, in every kind of organization, and with every type of human endeavor. This transformation is not to be compelled or controlled, but is something for which to wait and to pray, encouraged with both patience and love. Whatever else transformation does, it does not flow from you, but through you.

So be present in simplicity, be present with willingness, and be present with gratitude. More than anything, just be—for indeed, this *is* holiness, and this *is* blessing.

STEPS FOR BEING A

*In*asmuch as *it's more art than science, you'll hav*
and the lives of others. Following

1. OPEN YOURSELF.

Begin not with the other person but with you. Become present to yourself in a way that is honest, insightful, and accepting. Open to your uniqueness, humanness, prejudices, brokenness, and wholeness. Do this by owning your life story, continually fathoming who you are in a holistic manner, and developing or utilizing a support system to which you hold yourself accountable.

2. INTEND TO BE A HEALING PRESENCE.

Aware that healing presence doesn't just occur out of the blue, you intentionally decide to be such a presence with another. Intend to promote healing in its many forms, while being understanding of yourself as you emerge in the day-to-day intricacies of this practice.

3. PREPARE A SPACE FOR HEALING PRESENCE TO TAKE PLACE.

Clear a space to interact with the other or others, assuring as much privacy as possible and creating an atmosphere of calm. Prepare a space also within by placing your self out of the way and clearing away your personal expectations for what the other should be or do.

4. HONOR THE ONE IN YOUR CARE.

Approach those you accompany as people with dignity and worth. Show your regard for them by honoring their

HEALING PRESENCE

your own ways of bringing healing presence into your life
a rough order for how you might proceed.

individuality, equality, humanness, separateness, and sacredness.
Respect their natural and unique healing capacity.

5. OFFER WHAT YOU HAVE TO GIVE.

Freely and simply make available what you have to offer,
realizing it's up to the other or others to accept or not. Offer
presence, loving acceptance, empathy, dependability, an unselfish
focus on them, your firm belief in them, your willingness to follow
their lead, and, as much as anything, hope.

6. RECEIVE THE GIFTS THAT COME.

Accept with a grateful heart what is yours to receive. This may
include living your life more fully as a result of this practice. Other
gifts may include uncovering your genuine self, enjoying wonderful
relationships, finding personal satisfaction, realizing you have made
a difference, receiving your own healing, and exploring some of life's
most valuable lessons.

7. LIVE A LIFE OF WHOLENESS & BALANCE.

There is more to life than being a healing presence. So live
your days fully, caring for your own needs, setting appropriate
boundaries, encouraging your own growth, and nurturing a loving
attitude toward life, including the sacred dimension. Affirm and
live out the truth of the transforming potential of healing presence.
Be grateful for the possibilities.

Acknowledgements

From the time I first conceptualized this book, I knew I wanted to work with someone who could bring a fresh perspective to this work—a perspective similar enough to be complementary to mine, yet different enough to add its own unique dimension. So I asked Susan Cutshall and was grateful when she agreed. While I had an abiding respect for her sensitivity and her abilities as a hospice chaplain, group leader, and spiritual director, my respect grew into real admiration and deep appreciation for the generous, insightful spirit she brought to this project from beginning to end. She unselfishly shared her original ideas, her gathered expertise, her rich experience, and her thoughtful reflections at every phase of our work together. Through many months of planning, writing, and rewriting, she made herself available at all hours of the day and night as we communicated across three time zones, two professional settings, and one gender boundary, utilizing about every means of communication that modern technology could offer us. In many ways this is Susan's book as much as mine. More than collaborating *about* healing presence, she *was* healing presence throughout the process, and remains so still. I am significantly indebted to her.

Jinnie Draper was also present throughout the process, offering suggestions, sending articles, providing support all the way from Nova Scotia. She was particularly helpful during the final phases of writing as she provided extremely detailed and equally wise advice, always interlaced with her keen awareness of the spiritual dimension. Similarly, Debra Noell was a godsend during final editing as she stepped in to share her gifts both as a professional writer and therapist to help catch the many mistakes I made as a writer and thinker.

Many others gave of themselves in numerous ways, including offering insights, reading manuscripts, and providing encouragement. Susan and I wish to thank Clare Barton, Holly Book, Kathy Brita, Chris Crawford, Sue Devito, Martha Ebel, Khris Ford, John Gantt, Andrea Gould, Carrie Hackney, Ellen Hubbe, Ronna Jevne, Paul Johnson, Gail Kittleson, JoAnn Klink, Jennifer Levine, Ed Madara, Larry and Jerry Malmgren, Daphne Michaels, Bernie Miller, Christen Miller-Rieman, Kathleen O'Connor, Debra Peevy, John Peterson, Eldon Pickering, Claire Plourde, Jim Plourde, Lea Robinson, John Saynor,

Margaret Ann Schmidt, Art Schmidt, John Schneider, Christy Spencer, Jan Swope, and Rorry Zahourek. Appreciation is also due the participants in the "Soul of Practice" workshop at Hilton Head December 5-6, 2000 and especially the workshop leaders: Joan Klagsbrun and Tom Yeomans. Teri Marquart handled all the graphic design work for this book with her usual creativity and flair.

I must confess that there were times when the subject of this book seemed to elude me. How do you write about "being healing presence" in a helpful, practical way without resorting to writing about "doing healing presence"? Time after time I felt tempted to give up on this project, or at least delay it until another time in my life. Time after time the people I've acknowledged here—especially Susan—came forward and communicated, "This *is* worth doing." With their help, and *only* with their help, this book has come to be. I readily acknowledge that the limits of this book are mine. I also acknowledge that in those places where the book works, it is much more than my influence that made it possible. I am grateful to have experienced the generous support of such a far-flung yet intimate community of souls, healing presences all. I feel humbled they joined me.

James E. Miller is a counselor, spiritual director, writer/photographer, and lecturer who presents in the areas of healing presence, caregiving, spirituality, loss and grief, and managing transition. He is an ordained minister as well as the founder of Willowgreen Productions and Willowgreen Publishing in Fort Wayne, Indiana.

Susan C. Cutshall is a hospice chaplain and spiritual director with over thirty years experience in the areas of death and dying, health care, and feminine spirituality and ritual. Susan is an ordained minister in the United Church of Christ and is currently the Spiritual Care Coordinator with the Franciscan Hospice System in Tacoma, Washington.

VIDEOS BY JAMES E. MILLER

Invincible Summer
Listen to Your Sadness
How Do I Go On?
Nothing Is Permanent Except Change
By the Waters of Babylon
We Will Remember
Gaining a Heart of Wisdom
Awaken to Hope
Be at Peace
The Natural Way of Prayer
You Shall Not Be Overcome
The Grit and Grace of Being a Caregiver
Why Yellow?
Common Bushes Afire
When Mourning Dawns
All Seasons Shall Be Sweet
The Art of Listening in a Healing Way
Grief Has Its Seasons
My Times Are in Thy Hands
My Shepherd is the Lord
The Gift of Healing Presence
This Time of Caregiving

WILLOWGREEN

Willowgreen designs, creates, and markets printed books, e-books, audiobooks, videos, and web-based programs in the areas of caregiving, illness and dying, loss and grief, life transition, older age, spirituality, and hope. Willowgreen materials always blend advancing knowledge with artful presentation, psychological and spiritual truth with timeless wisdom, appreciation for the commonplace with openness to the sacred. The goal of each Willowgreen resource is to be healing in and of itself, more than just a resource about healing.

For our latest catalog contact

Willowgreen

10351 Dawson's Creek Boulevard, Suite B

Fort Wayne, Indiana 46825

260/490-2222

jmiller@willowgreen. com

www. willowgreen. com